COMPLETE ✶ FICTION

Prompts to Ignite Your Imagination!

This edition published by Piccadilly (USA) Inc.

10 9 8 7 6 5 4 3 2 1

Made in China

ISBN: 978-1-48897-518-9

THIS BELONGS TO

COMPLETE ✷ FICTION

Do you love to write? Are you ready to challenge yourself like never before? How well do you write fictional stories?

Fiction beckons a writer to explore the deepest recesses of their creative mind, for the world and story they create is born entirely from imagination. Fiction demands originality and inventiveness. It requires the meticulous crafting of a narrative that transcends the bounds of reality, opening doors to uncharted territories and endless possibilities. Whereas non-fiction is anchored in facts and truth.

Our "Complete Fiction" story-crafting guide is your gateway to crafting compelling and innovative short stories. Within these pages, you will find an array of vibrant and thought-provoking prompts designed to ignite your creativity. Every prompt serves as a stepping stone, guiding you to construct a storyline that is uniquely your own pushing the limits of your imaginativeness.

In fiction, there are no rules—only the ones you choose to follow. Every blank page is a portal—an open invitation to defy logic, reinvent reality, and explore what could be, not just what is. This space gives you permission to dream loudly and without apology. You're not just writing stories; you're breathing life into characters, building landscapes from scratch, and shaping plot twists that nobody sees coming. Fiction isn't bound by the rules of the real world—it dares you to break them. Here, the impossible becomes the foundation for something unforgettable.

What makes fiction so powerful is its ability to reflect truth through imagination. Behind every magical spell or dystopian city is a piece of the human spirit—a fear, a hope, a what-if. And when you tap into that emotional core, your storytelling becomes more than entertainment—it becomes transformative. The more you trust your creativity, the more you'll surprise yourself. These stories are yours to build, one vivid sentence at a time

Each prompt is paired with vivid, inspiring artwork, designed to immerse you in the story you're conjuring. Let these visual guides transport you into the heart of your fictional tale as you write it. Explore all the sub-genres of fiction, from fantasy to scientific or from mythology to magic. Journey beyond the ordinary and into the extraordinary, where your imagination knows no bounds.

"Complete Fiction" allows you, the writer, to break free from the constraints of the familiar, and venture into realms of your own creation, breaking the barriers of reality. So, take a deep breath, open your mind, and flex your creative writing muscles. Show off your originality one story at a time, and transform these prompts into one-of-a-kind, unique, masterpieces.

✷ Warm-Up Exercise: Break the Rules First

Before you dive into the prompts ahead, take a moment to wake up your imagination. Think of this as your creative stretch—no pressure, just play.

Write a short scene (half a page or less) where one rule of reality no longer applies. Maybe gravity only works when you're smiling. Maybe people swap memories when they make eye contact. Maybe words are no longer spoken—they appear as glowing shapes in the air.

Your mission:

- Introduce a character who is navigating this new reality for the first time.
- Focus less on logic, more on mood and movement.
- Don't edit. Don't overthink. Just let the scene unfold.

Let your creativity run wild—this isn't about perfection, it's about unlocking possibility. When you're done, turn the page and begin crafting fiction that only you could write.

I waited until the last minute to get my Christmas shopping done, and now the mall is so crowded that I can't even move. The stores close in 15 minutes, and I still have two gifts left to buy. Unexpectedly, I heard a loud bell ring three times. As I made a mad dash towards my last stop, I noticed everyone was frozen. It was like time had stopped, but I was still moving.

The audience was on their feet dancing and singing. My bestie and I were screaming in disbelief, we were at the concert of our favorite band. We had waited forever for this moment and now their best song would be the encore. We were lost in the music when we felt a strange sensation come over us. Suddenly, I noticed the band members removing what appeared to be human masks, only to unveil what looked like alien life forms.

It was a beautiful day at the park, perfect for feeding pigeons and people-watching. All of a sudden, I saw a dark shadow skulking through the trees. It was a nondescript shape, almost like a blob, and I couldn't tell what it was. I noticed it was making its way closer to the playground where the children were. I stood up to get a better look, but it moved fast, like smoke in the wind. It seemed to grow larger the closer it got to the park. Then, out of nowhere, I heard a group of kids screaming.

The twins were finally asleep, and my adventures in babysitting would soon be over when the Robinsons got back from the theatre. I sat down to finish my homework; it was due Monday, and I didn't need an incomplete in Physics. I dozed off halfway through the chapter on quantum mechanics, only to be woken by an odd buzzing sound coming from the garage. I checked on the kids to make sure they weren't playing a prank on me, but they were sound asleep. As I crept downstairs, moving closer to the garage, the sound grew louder, almost like hordes of bees swarming. Out of nowhere, I felt a prick on my neck and began to black out.

My alarm was blaring, and as I reached to turn it off, I couldn't open my eyes. I tried to wipe them, and that's when I felt something sticky and thick like glue. I couldn't get it off no matter how hard I rubbed. I started to panic, and that's when I felt the same substance begin covering my feet...

The hurricane was approaching, and we were bracing for impact. When the storm hit, gale-force winds flung my front door open. My dog ran outside, terrified, and as I chased after him, I was thrown into a power line by the storm's fury. I didn't notice it right away, but I had a massive bump on my head from the collision. A few minutes later, I felt a strange pulsing through my body, and then...

Rumor has it there's an elusive cave that only appears at certain times of the day. The sun and moon must be at the perfect location; otherwise, it's camouflaged. I decided to assemble a group of avid spelunkers to help me search for this hidden cave. I couldn't wait to discover what secrets it might hold.

As I was walking home from school, I noticed a furry black cat with hypnotizing green eyes following me. After walking halfway home, I looked back, and the cat was still trotting along behind me. As I approached my house, I noticed the cat was gone, but when I turned back around, 100 black cats were sitting in my front yard. The closer I got to my door, the more their green eyes began to glow.

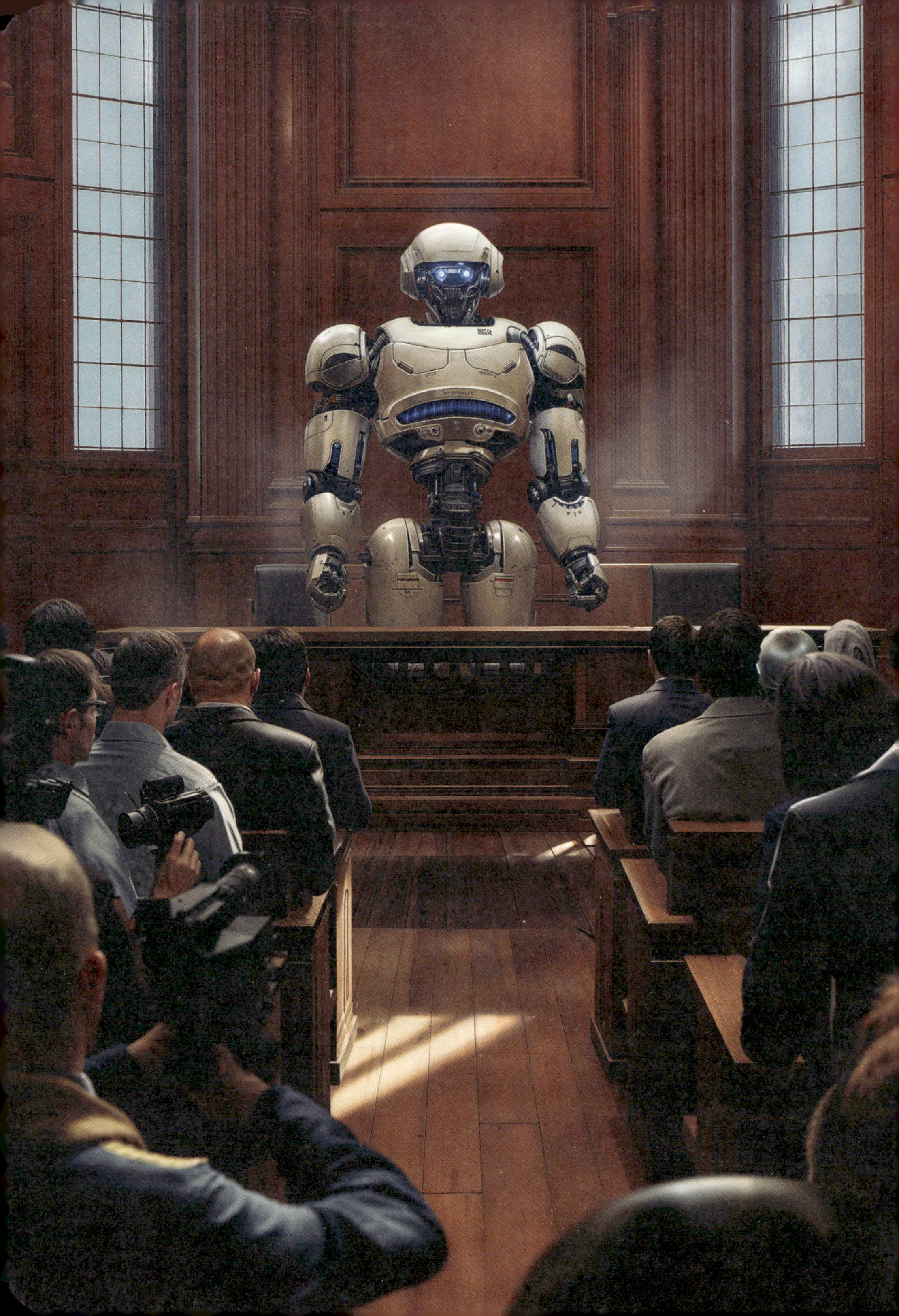

I was one of the many reporters waiting for the verdict. The trial had gained worldwide attention, and everyone was on the edge of their seat. If the defendant was found guilty, they would be the first person sentenced to the new robot rehabilitation program. Finally, the jury was back, and the future of our criminal justice system hung in the balance. How much power were we prepared to give the machines?

It was a hard-fought chess tournament, but I prevailed. Every match was challenging and exhausting, but I was ecstatic at the thought of finally being awarded the title of Grandmaster. Exhausted, I just crawled into bed; I didn't even feel like eating. Minutes later, I was surrounded by chess pieces that were alive. Knights, rooks, and bishops were charging toward me. I looked down, and the ground was a giant chessboard. Was I dreaming, or was this an alternate reality? I heard a battle cry in the distance, and there they were—the King and Queen.

We boarded the plane for a long-awaited vacation. I was planning on taking a nap for the 5-hour flight. I dozed off, only to be awakened by the plane shaking violently. I looked out the window and saw grotesque, gargoyle-like creatures mounted on the wings of the aircraft. It felt like a scene out of the Twilight Zone, but nobody could have predicted what would happen next.

Here I was, stranded on an unfamiliar, desolate road with a flat tire. In the distance, I heard a howl that sounded like the moan of an injured animal. I didn't want to stick around to find out what it was, but I was stuck. I had no cell service and no way to get help. To make matters worse, the sound kept getting louder, as if it was moving closer. Then I got a whiff of blood, fresh blood, and before I knew it...

My favorite time of year, the beginning of autumn, was upon us, and I decided to show my children the pumpkin patch I frequented as a child. A peculiar old man was running the farm now. He seemed sweet and, oddly enough, resembled a gnome. I told him about the stories from my childhood and how special this place was to me. He suggested we select the fairytale pumpkins because they were magical and brought to life the spirit of the season. When we took the pumpkins home, we never imagined what would happen when we began carving them.

I was out for my normal run in Central Park. It was a brisk winter day, and I didn't have a care in the world. Halfway through my jog, I tripped over a branch, and as I picked myself up, I noticed four large black Clydesdale horses surrounding me. They were beautiful but terrifying, and before I could react...

My dad fancied himself an inventor and was always tinkering with something. He usually had two or three projects going at any given time. My mom always encouraged him, but he never hit pay dirt—at least not yet. One afternoon, when I came home from school, Dad called me into his workshop and showed me his latest invention. I laughed and told him it looked like a regular pair of glasses. He told me to put them on, and when I did...

The scales were starting to spread all over me. They had moved from my legs to my arms, and I no longer looked human. What was I becoming, and what had caused this transformation? I was beginning to shiver; I felt cold from head to toe. I knew I shouldn't look in the mirror, but I needed to see my reflection. Then I caught a glance of myself and...

MAGIC CASTLE

It's my brother's birthday, and he loves magic, so we surprised him by having his party at the Magic Castle. The Great Santini was performing, and his acts are famous for being mind-bending. My family volunteered me to go on stage and help with one of his tricks. Santini wanted to hypnotize me, and like a good sport, I agreed. After the show, it felt like I was still floating; everything seemed like a dream. I thought I was feeling the aftereffects of hypnosis, but then I started to...

The farmer told me I could pick apples from any of his trees except the golden apple tree. My curiosity got the better of me, and I became obsessed with tasting the golden apples. Why were they off-limits? They looked like the best apples in the orchard. When he left, I couldn't help myself; I ran over and took a few. They're just apples—what could it harm? I took a big bite, and then...

The weather conditions were ideal for skiing The Flying Dutchman. Newly fallen snow had created fresh powder, perfect for racing down the slopes. My friends and I were having a blast; it was exhilarating. Without warning, it started warming up, and the snow became slushy, making it very dangerous. We tried making our way to a safe part of the slopes, but in a flash, the ground gave way beneath us. We were falling down what appeared to be a dark ice portal. It grew colder by the moment, and we could hear the earth rumble around us.

We all heard stories about the mysterious white van. Everyone was on high alert—who would go missing next? The police didn't have any leads and weren't sharing much information with the public about the case. All the parents in the neighborhood came together to form a neighborhood watch group. We would take shifts, day and night, to protect our children and each other. Late one Thursday night, I was patrolling with a few others when I heard a scream over the walkie-talkie, "It's the white van, and whatever's driving it is not human!"

My dog would not stop barking, so I checked the cameras, but I didn't see anything. This was out of character for him; Peanut was a well-behaved dog. He was trying to warn me or protect me from something, but what? As I looked out the window, I noticed my home was engulfed in what appeared to be spiderwebs. They looked thick, sticky, and too big to have been created by a normal spider. Reluctantly, I opened my front door and immediately regretted it.

I was on my second bag of popcorn, waiting for my nephew to come up to bat. The score was tied, and things were serious; this was the Little League playoffs, after all. Out of the blue, a perfectly sunny day turned into a nightmare. It grew dark, the sky erupted, and it looked as if it was on fire. The crowd was crying in fear as soot and ash rained down on us. It was then that I looked up and saw...

He was a cute little frog, and I had seen him hopping around my garden for a few days. One afternoon, while pulling weeds, I felt something wet touch my hand. It was the frog; he had hopped over to say hi. He reminded me of the fairy tale "The Frog Prince," but then I became sad at the realization that I was alone. The whole encounter had me reeling, and then I thought, what the heck—if a princess can kiss a frog, then I can too! I was desperate, but if it meant finding true love, then it was worth it. I closed my eyes and leaned in to kiss the frog...

The avalanche had unearthed a massive creature with features resembling a woolly mammoth combined with a Sasquatch. It looked as if it had been frozen for centuries. When news spread about the discovery, scientists from all corners of the globe flocked to the mountain, hoping for the chance to examine the beast. A team was assembled, and as they began chipping away at the ice...

Frustrated, I was about to smash my project on the floor when I decided to give the formula another try. I had to win the senior science fair; I needed the prize money for college. As I carefully combined each ingredient, a gradual bubbling began, which was a good sign. In the blink of an eye, the bubbling grew out of control and dripped off my desk onto my teddy bear, Thomas. I started cleaning up the mess when I noticed Thomas start moving.

It was another great day on the fairway, and I was about to take my golf game to the next level. After a stressful week, I was finally relaxing. I reared back to swing when I heard a frightful grumbling beneath me. Then, without warning, the ground split open right in front of me. My caddy and I were on opposite sides of a 10-foot-wide crack that was infinitely deep and stretched for miles. Within seconds after the rupture, we were surrounded by flying insects the size of cats.

She looked back and saw the foxes chasing her—there had to be at least twenty or more. She had no idea why they were charging after her or if they meant her any harm, but she was too afraid to find out. After a half hour of running, she came to a cliff that dropped off into the river below. She would have to stand her ground against the foxes or take her chances and jump.

Instantaneously, it was like our quiet little township had become the center of a media circus. The mysterious castle being built had the masses buzzing with curiosity. The style of this mansion felt straight out of a storybook but with a hint of Gothic folklore. The secretive owner even created a man-made moat, making it harder to see inside the castle. It was like a time warp to a different era. Our once peaceful town had a new resident, and nobody knew anything about this recluse until one day when they...

I was taking this creative writing course with the hopes of learning something or at least becoming a better writer. The teacher told us to write with pen and paper so we could feel the words, but as usual, I was drawing a blank. Then I remembered my grandfather used to write for a newspaper—he said the typewriter brought his articles to life. I decided to grab it from the attic and give it a try. As I began typing, I could instantly see the appeal and understand why he loved it. Toward the end of my first page, something strange happened—the typewriter started typing on its own.

My boyfriend and I were taking a picturesque road trip to a bed and breakfast nestled in the countryside. Part of the destination's appeal was the gorgeous landscapes you'd see along the drive up there. Some of nature's most beautiful scenery was on display. Charming farms were spread out amongst the passing fields. Out of nowhere, we saw a terrifying scarecrow that seemed out of place for such a peaceful setting. After our shock subsided, we wrote it off as a bad joke. Then we began seeing the same scarecrow over and over for the next 10 miles. It wasn't a coincidence; it was unrealistic that all these farms would have the same horrifying scarecrow. Then the scarecrow started appearing every mile, and it felt like...

When I got home from school, I was in a bad mood—everyone had forgotten my birthday. Then I saw a package from my favorite aunt, who was an archaeologist and traveled the world. I tore open the gift, thankful she thought of me—it appeared to be an old book. She left me a note telling me to be careful while reading it because it belonged to a powerful pharaoh. Her team had accidentally uncovered it during an expedition in Egypt. I started reading but noticed it was filled with hieroglyphics that I didn't understand. As I scrolled through each page, my room abruptly began...

One day, while out running errands, I stumbled upon a cute antique store filled with treasures. While shopping, I found a beautiful sword that looked like it could belong to King Arthur. My dad's birthday was around the corner, so I decided to buy it for him. He collected antiques and would love it. While driving back home, I heard an unusual humming coming from the back seat where I had put the sword. The further away I got from the antique store, the louder the sound became until...

My dog was gone, and I was in shock. I began plastering the neighborhood with "Missing Dog" posters, hoping someone would find and return her. She was not only my dog but my best friend, and it was unlike her to run away. A few days later, there was a knock at the door—it was my dog, just sitting on the front porch. I was overjoyed, but then I immediately began checking her for injuries. That's when I spotted the stitches above her ears.

The world was in the middle of a phenomenon. Roosters across the globe, from coast to coast and in every country, had begun crowing in unison. Every day, each hour on the hour, roosters everywhere began cock-a-doodling. Farmers were in an uproar, and scientists couldn't explain it. The constant crowing set off a negative chain of events and threw off the balance of nature. Soon, other animals began...

I was glued to the TV; the season finale was finally here, but before the climactic ending, the television screen went solid black. All of a sudden, green lines appeared to be dancing on the screen, accompanied by different frequencies of sound. I went from being agitated to feeling like I was in a trance. A few minutes later...

Hillside Estates was the most beautiful wine vineyard in all of California. Their award-winning hybrid grapes produced some of the most sophisticated wines in the world. Recently, trouble was reported on the estate, and rumors of vines growing uncontrollably have been circulating in Sonoma County. A few inspectors from the state have gone missing while investigating these dangerous conditions, and now...

Our identities were being stolen, and it felt like humanity was slowly being erased. AXIS, a rogue group of hackers, wanted to wreak havoc on society. They had written a program that allowed them to control new AI technology. People's voices, photos, and even mannerisms were being duplicated, making humans useless in this technologically advanced society. This was just the beginning; things were getting worse...

My grandpa and I had been hunting for treasures since I was little. It was our way of spending time together, and he would tell me stories from yesteryear. We usually explored parks, our lake house, and mostly just around the neighborhood. However, today would be our first time using our metal detector at the beach. After an hour of scavenging, I finally got a signal. Grandpa and I began to dig feverishly, then I pulled up a bronze necklace with an onyx center. Excited, I showed Grandpa, but he was frozen in shock, and all he could say was, "She's back."

My cat would not come into the house. She was petrified, almost like she sensed danger. She began hissing and growling. Then the hair on her back stood up, but I didn't see or hear anything. Out of the corner of my eye, I caught a shadow and what appeared to be a massive reptilian tail. Then I heard glass shatter...

I was invited to attend a séance by my next-door neighbor. She knew I had lost my best friend and thought it would make me feel better if I made contact. When I arrived, there were a few other people, all wanting to reach out to someone. The medium performing the ceremony asked us to join hands and place something from our loved ones on the table. She began chanting, and without warning, things started to move around in the room. She asked us to remain calm, but it was getting worse. Suddenly, the medium shouted, "Oh no, it crossed over and it's in the room!"

Fishermen were reporting their catch of oysters coming up covered in a strange black substance they couldn't identify. Nobody could pry the oysters open; the foreign matter seemed to have cemented them shut. Some of the oysters were collected and sent to marine biologists at the university. After careful examination, they determined the oysters were...

The neighborhood bullies were at it again, and this time they were attacking an elderly man who usually kept to himself. They teased him mercilessly and threw trash at him on his own lawn. What those mean kids didn't know was that the old man they were taunting was a warlock. He was capable of great power but had stopped using it as he grew older. After the bullies had their fun at his expense, they headed to an amusement park, unaware that the sorcerer was following closely behind them.

For Charlotte's 18th birthday, her mother gave her a letter from her great-grandfather. The letter would change her life and uncover buried family secrets. She was instructed to travel to Galveston Island and meet a historian named Ruth. There, she would learn about her family's legacy and their connection to the famous pirate Jean Lafitte.

One day at work, multiple voices began surrounding me. Some were shouting, and some were in different languages, but none of them sounded like my voice. Initially, I thought I was losing my mind, but then I realized I was able to hear other people's thoughts. I tried my best to tune it out, but it was difficult. Then the unthinkable happened. I was grabbing lunch at the office cafeteria when I heard a voice planning a murder. This person wanted to kill their spouse and was trying to work up the courage to do it. One of my co-workers was about to attempt the perfect crime.

I decided to stay home from work today. All I wanted to do was sleep. Then, out of the blue, I heard a boom and then another boom—loud, consecutive, thunderous booms. I peeked out my window and saw my neighbors screaming and pointing. The noise sounded like it was getting closer, so reluctantly, I went outside. It was then I noticed all the trees were exploding one by one.

The fog was so thick I couldn't see the road in front of me. I thought about pulling over, but I just wanted to get home. I slowed my speed, hoping to avoid a collision, but the fog kept growing thicker. It was taking shape right before my eyes, swirling around like a tornado but without the wind. Before I knew it, the fog had taken shape and looked like nothing I'd ever seen. Slowly, it began reaching for me right through the windshield...

The air had a foul stench of decomposition. The odor was all around me, but I couldn't find anything decaying. Uncertain why my home smelled like death, I decided to get someone to check under my house. The contractors wanted to dig around the foundation and check for a sewer leak, but I never anticipated they would discover...

Henry loved to make hand puppets. His class was having a "show and tell" day, and he wanted to entertain the students. Henry hoped to design a play that showcased all his puppets, but he was drawing a blank. He went to bed feeling sad, worried everyone would make fun of him. The puppets were so grateful Henry created them that they wanted to surprise him by giving him the ultimate puppet show. The next day at school, Henry was shocked when he saw his puppets...

The king was in another one of his moods, and I was sent to cheer him up. My job was a deadly one; as the court jester, if I didn't make the king laugh or bring him joy, I would lose my head. Trembling at the thought of being beheaded and out of jokes, I needed to think quickly. I had used all the props in the castle, so I was looking for something new. I journeyed deep into the forest and met with a wizard. I offered to trade gold coins for a potion that would make the king happy. Unaware of the wizard's true intentions for the king, I made the exchange. The next day, I gave the king the potion, but then...

Writing a children's book has always been my dream. I loved books as a kid; they kept me company when I was alone. I wanted the next generation to have books similar to the ones I loved but with a twist. I grabbed all the books from my childhood and began reading them again for inspiration. After a while, I fell asleep at my desk, reading about fairies and princesses, only to be awakened by the soft sounds of giggling. With my head still on my desk, I opened the corner of my eye, and to my surprise, I saw three little fairies with wands floating above me.

Tommy desperately wanted to play basketball, but being a paraplegic had its limitations. He knew he would never dunk on his own; his legs wouldn't allow it. Desperate to find freedom from his prison, better known as his wheelchair, Tommy worked day and night on his magic shoes. He wanted to invent shoes that allowed other kids like himself to have the ability to fly, even if only for a short time. He was trying to combine jet engines with shoes but on a smaller scale. His invention was almost completed when something unexpected happened...

The North Pole was in an uproar. It was 23 days until Christmas, and one of the elves had lost Santa's "naughty list." Santa wanted to complete the map of his final route but couldn't do it without the list. The head elf suspected someone was hiding it on purpose, and he needed to come up with a plan to catch the culprit before Christmas was ruined.

The residents of the small town were panicked—crows were everywhere. They lined the streets and buildings; it felt like every crow far and wide had descended on them. The church elder shouted, "Crows are an omen of death; the plague is upon us!"

The Smiths had just given birth to their first child. Mom and baby were doing well, and the entire family was thrilled. In an instant, the ground trembled, the electricity flickered, and ambulance sirens were ringing. Everyone thought it was an earthquake, but in room 206 at Mercy General Hospital, Lisa and Todd Smith received some surprising visitors. Three large angels appeared before them and warned the new parents that their child was in danger and needed to come with them.

I didn't know my grandparents very well. They lived in another country, and we seldom visited. Their home was old-fashioned and had ornate clocks in every room. My grandmother told me each clock was special and had a unique history, but the clocks looked scary to me. After dinner, as we prepared for bed, she told me never to come out of my room after 11 p.m. At midnight, all the clock bells began ringing and didn't stop. A few minutes later, the noise was driving me crazy. Something weird was going on, so I snuck out of the room against my grandmother's instructions. That's when I saw my grandparents doing the unthinkable...

Red Xs were being left all over the city—on power lines, bus stops, and signs everywhere. Each morning, there were fresh bright red Xs in new locations around town, and to make matters worse, no one had seen anything. People were clueless as to who was leaving their mark and why. There was speculation it was graffiti connected to gang turf disputes, but the countdown had begun, and by midnight everything would be revealed.

The time had come for young Sonara to return to her home planet of Jungara. She had been hidden on Earth from enemy tribes that wanted to eradicate her Amazonian bloodline. The elders were waiting to train her to defend her true home. Sonara's adoptive parents explained everything and revealed the secrets they had kept to protect her. Now that she was older, it was time for her to return to her planet. Sonara was distraught at the thought of leaving her life on Earth behind. She refused to become a warrior in a place she knew nothing about. That night, she packed a bag and ran away, unaware that galaxy bounty hunters were looking for her.

Two little penguins showed up on my doorstep, which was odd because penguins aren't native to where I live. They were making honking sounds and flapping as if they needed help. It seemed like they wanted me to follow them, so I did. They led me through the woods behind my neighborhood and down a trail that led to the beach. As we approached the shore, the penguins reacted hysterically, and then I understood why they were so desperate.

Dogs kept disappearing from my neighborhood at an alarming rate, too many to be a coincidence. I love a good mystery, so I decided to look into it. I set up surveillance in subdivisions where owners could afford a ransom if their dog was snatched. It didn't take long for me to spot something fishy. Two huge figures came out of the shadows and snatched a poodle while I was watching. They loaded the dog into a van and took off, but I was following close behind them...

Mary had been a zookeeper for over 10 years and loved all the animals she worked with, but she shared a special bond with a gorilla named Koko. She'd been working with Koko for a year now and was convinced Koko was different. One day, while Mary was working with all the apes at the zoo, she noticed Koko building something with toys. Koko motioned for Mary to come over. When Mary looked at the display, it was clear that Koko was trying to tell her something very serious.

My new neighbor gives me the creeps. He comes and goes at strange hours of the day, and there are always weird noises coming from his basement. I was afraid of him, but my curiosity and concern got the better of me. I decided to get a closer look at what he was doing the next time he left. It was about 10 p.m. when I saw my neighbor drive off with two large bags. That was my cue to start snooping, so I made my way to his backyard as quietly as I could. I found a small window that gave me a peek into his basement, and I saw what appeared to be...

Tyler received a 3D printer for Christmas and initially, he wasn't happy. He had begged his parents for the latest gaming system, but they wanted him to focus on more educational pursuits. He had been staring at that printer for days with resentment in his eyes, but then he had an evil genius moment. Tyler decided he could make money using the printer, but his idea was not very legitimate. He grabbed as much silly putty, latex, and modeling clay as he could find and began creating...

Somebody was leaving cryptic messages around the university. At first, it started as a riddle, and students thought it was a joke, but then the tone began to sound desperate and more sinister. Randomly, cipher codes started appearing in the college paper, on flyers around campus, and one cipher was even burned into the grass on the quad. The students decided to hold a conference to discuss recent events, and that's when...

I was so confused by my dream and needed answers. Then I remembered the mysterious gypsy woman who told me this would happen. She said I would visit her when the time was right. Now she's all I can think about; maybe she holds the key. I felt a strange pull urging me to visit her caravan and explore the meaning behind my dream. When I knocked on her door, she replied, "Come in, I've been waiting for you, dear."

There's a new artist in the Chelsea District of New York, and I have been dying to get tickets to his next exhibition, but it's completely sold out. Luckily, I have a connection, and I can't wait to attend. The reviews from his last show proclaimed the event as otherworldly, exotic, and intense. As I entered the gallery, it felt like his paintings were alive. Walking around, one particular piece caught my eye. I was captivated; it was like his work had put a spell on me. I was being pulled into the art piece—literally. Was it magic? Was he human? What was happening to me?

I kept experiencing the same day over and over. Even though my clothes changed and the things I said, the places I ate, and what I did were different, it seemed like I was stuck in a loop. I felt like a glitch in a computer program, and to compound the problem, I wasn't always cognizant it was happening. It seemed as though something was erasing my memories and impeding my lucidity. After days of feeling like I was stuck on a hamster wheel, bits and pieces of my memory began to return, and then everything made sense.

I hated living in a small town. In addition to it being boring, the rumor mill was always swirling. Parents would create ridiculously scary urban legends to scare kids into behaving well. The teenagers caught on to their schemes and usually turned the terrorizing tales into pranks. It was September, which meant the start of another school year and another urban legend the parents would spin into circulation. My first thought was to shake my head when I heard the myth, but for some reason, this one felt different, like there could be some truth to it. It was about the old sawmill at the edge of town and why it really closed down.

Sabrina was building a sandcastle on the beach when a rogue wave hit the shore hard, sweeping her out into the ocean. Within an instant, young Sabrina was struggling to stay above water, but the current was too strong and pulled her under. Just when she thought she would drown, something grabbed her. The figure looked like a mermaid but was different from what she'd seen in storybooks. Sabrina was underwater but encased in a bubble and able to breathe. They swam together for a few minutes, but when the mermaid reached out her hand to Sabrina...

2

Everyone was talking about the fire ant invasion this season. Normally, we see ant mounds start popping up at the start of spring, but here we are in the heart of winter, and they are multiplying in the snow. I wasn't worried about it yet since we didn't go outside much in the cold, but my neighbor was frustrated. One day, he came over waving a $300 bill from the extermination company he'd paid to have the ants eradicated, but the mounds were still everywhere. I decided I might need to take a closer look because I hadn't seen any actual ants. I went to the mound near my mailbox, and as I bent down, I noticed a camera lens buried in the mound.

An interesting man came to visit us at school today. He was our special guest speaker, and I don't know if he was trying to get our attention or if his story was true, but it stuck with me. He stated that the secret to life was hidden among the bees. He didn't go into much detail about what he meant, other than to say how important bees were to our ecosystem, especially to humans. I couldn't shake what he said to us about the bees. He looked right at me when he said it; it felt like a challenge, so I knew I had to...

Luna's grandmother wanted to teach her a special recipe that had been passed down through the tribe over the years. This recipe was created by an elder medicine woman more than 300 years ago who had favor with "The Great Spirit." Luna's grandmother explained the importance of the recipe and how it was to be kept secret. The recipe was for healing and protection against Skin-walkers. She warned Luna that should the recipe fall into the hands of the wrong person, their entire tribe would be in grave danger. One day, as Luna tried to prepare the recipe for the upcoming ceremony, a great wind blew...

The Harpers had just closed on their dream home. It was a fixer-upper, but they didn't mind and were looking forward to making it their own style. It was the couple's first night in their new home, and they wanted to get a good night's sleep so they could meet with renovators early in the morning. An hour later, they heard a crash come from downstairs. Mr. Harper inspected the entire house, and everything seemed fine. Minutes later, a loud organ began playing, all the mirrors shattered, and doors were opening and closing. The couple began running toward the front door, and that's when...

She traveled to the secret mountain in preparation for the ritual. She had to try and resurrect her father in the hope it could save her village from the same sorcerer who killed him. She had gained the help of a powerful onmyōji to guide her through the process. She waited for the moon to be at its fullest, prepared the ingredients, and placed the sacrifice in the center of the stone. As she began the ceremony, a voice taunted her from the shadows...

Patti was the most adored hippo at the animal rehab center. Despite a serious injury from another hippo, her sweet disposition charmed everyone who met her. She especially loved her daily feedings of fresh watermelon, and the crew always looked forward to treating her. But today, something was off. A rogue scientist had infiltrated the facility with malice on his mind. He'd laced Patti's melons with an experimental serum—one designed to weaponize hippos. Unaware, Patti began gobbling one melon after the next, juice dribbling down her chin as the crew cheered her on. Then she paused. And that's when everything started to change.

We had finally made it to Hawaii for our romantic getaway. My fiancé Jeff, an avid hiker, was thrilled to tour the island's largest volcano. I, on the other hand, was the cautious one—more beach chair than trail shoes—and begged him to let me relax by the ocean instead. But Jeff nudged my sense of adventure, and soon we were hiking the rugged terrain, rewarded with insanely beautiful views of the island. Just as I started to think maybe this wasn't such a bad idea, I heard Jeff scream one word that turned my blood cold: "Run."

Taking surfing lessons had always been on my bucket list. I've always loved the ocean, and grabbing a board to explore the waves felt like the perfect way to experience it from a new perspective. After a few lessons, I started to get the hang of it—like I was a natural. One sunny afternoon, as I caught a wave and rode it in, I noticed a shadow just beneath the surface of the water. My mind instantly screamed shark, but when I caught another glimpse, I realized it was something else—massive, ancient, and almost prehistoric in shape. I paddled hard, heart racing, but then the water beneath me began to rise...

The wind had picked up, and a sudden gust jerked my kite hard, yanking the string from my hand. Before I knew it, I was sprinting after it, chasing the runaway kite as it soared and dipped wildly. As the wind finally began to die down, the kite drifted into the nearby woods and got caught among the treetops. Lucky for me, the string was long enough that I could still reach it. I jumped, stretched my arms, and caught the tail—only to realize I was now dangling off the ground. I tried to free it from the branches, but before I could untangle it, the string went taut and began to rise, pulling me higher, toward something moving in the canopy above.

It started as a joke—naming the orphaned skunk I rescued "Rainbows" because of the strange, iridescent stripes running down its back. But the more time I spent with it, the more I realized something wasn't normal. Rainbows never ate, never slept, and glowed faintly at night like something radioactive. At first, I thought my eyes were playing tricks on me—until the grass where it walked began to shimmer and change colors. One morning, I stepped outside to find the entire backyard glowing in streaks of violet, gold, and green. That's when I noticed a trail of tiny gold paw prints leading toward the open field, and when I followed them, I found Rainbows...

While picking wildflowers in the woods behind my grandparents' old farmhouse, I stumbled upon a massive, gnarled tree with a hollowed-out trunk. As I paused to gather a few more blooms, I heard something faint—a whisper. I leaned in closer, and that's when I heard it clearly: someone calling for help from deep inside the hole in the tree. I dropped to my knees and peered into the darkness, calling back, but no one answered. Then the whisper came again, louder this time. I reached in slowly, fingers brushing against something soft... and then it moved.

The desert sun was brutal, and I had nearly given up hope of finding shelter when I spotted a strange cactus—tall, glowing faintly, and pulsing as if it were breathing. As I reached out to touch it, the cactus split open down the center, revealing a swirling portal inside. I took a cautious step closer, but the ground suddenly trembled beneath me as a massive creature burst from the sand. It was a giant snake, and its eyes locked on me. I stumbled backward toward the cactus unsure which danger was worse... but then the portal began to pull me in.

Deep in the hills behind the old, abandoned church was a mine we were always told to stay away from. Of course, that only made it more tempting. One afternoon, I slipped through the rusted gate and made my way inside, flashlight flickering against damp rock walls. As I turned a corner, the floor gave way beneath me, dropping me into a narrow tunnel I didn't recognize. That's when I heard voices—gruff and muttering. I crept forward and peeked around a jagged wall to see a group of gnomes huddled around a pile of gold. One of them stopped, lifted its head, and sniffed the air. "We're not alone," it growled—and suddenly, I was running for my life when...

The hot air balloon ride was supposed to be peaceful—just a quiet sunrise float above the coastline. I leaned over the edge of the basket, enjoying the view, when a pelican swooped in out of nowhere and landed beside me, completely unbothered by my shock. At first, I laughed, thinking it was just a bold bird looking for a place to rest. But then it began pecking at my bag of popcorn, tearing it open and flinging kernels into the wind. That's when more pelicans started circling overhead, drawn in by the scent—then balloon began to tilt...

The abandoned city, once home to a network of chemical plants, had been sealed off for decades—its crumbling streets and rusting towers left to rot. We were sent below, into the sewer system that ran beneath it, to assess what remained of the old infrastructure. Then we heard it: a strange fluttering sound, like wings brushing against concrete. At first, we thought it was rats or maybe bats, until a massive shadow passed over our headlamps. Out of the darkness came a swarm of giant moth-like creatures, their wings wide and silent, their eyes glowing dimly in the dark. One by one, our lights went out—then the screaming started...

It was just another late night at the office, crunching numbers and finishing reports long after everyone else had gone home. As I went to lock up, I noticed a dusty briefcase tucked behind the supply cabinet—one I'd never seen before. Curiosity got the better of me. I popped the latches open and froze. Inside were neat stacks of cash, bundled tightly and packed to the brim. No note, no ID, just money. Lots of it. That's when I heard the elevator ding, followed by a deep voice behind me: "The alarm on the briefcase was triggered."

Strawberry Festival Day had finally arrived, and Grandma Judy was practically buzzing with excitement to show off her new strawberry cake. But her decades-long rival, Matilda Swanson, had entered the contest too—and that meant war. Grandma had tasked me with keeping an eye on Matilda, certain she'd try one of her usual tricks. As I trailed her through the crowd toward the dessert display cases, that's when I saw Matilda...

No one believed the rumors at first—tales of aggressive hornets swarming the edges of town and monarch butterflies gathering in unusual, almost strategic formations. People said it was climate change or early migration, but I wasn't so sure. I saw them with my own eyes: monarchs moving in tight patterns, diving at hornets mid-air like they were defending something. By the end of the week, the power flickered across town, crops looked shredded, and the skies above us were a blur of wings. Our small town had become the battleground for something we didn't understand—and it was only getting worse...

It started as a harmless internet challenge—an augmented reality filter that turned people into cartoon versions of themselves. At first, it was fun. Everyone shared videos of big eyes, exaggerated smiles, and stretchy limbs. But then, some people stopped changing back. Their voices grew higher, their skin smoother, their movements less...human. I watched in horror as my neighbor's face froze in a permanent grin, her hands puffed into oversized gloves. No one knew how to reverse it, and the transformation was spreading fast. I looked in the mirror and saw my reflection begin to flicker—then warp.

It started subtly in the quaint neighborhood of Charming Oaks—a mailbox missing here, another one gone there. Most neighbors blamed pranksters or local kids, but I knew better. Every night, just past midnight, I saw him: a tall, cloaked man moving silently from yard to yard, methodically removing mailboxes like they were ticking time bombs. He never rushed, never looked around, just vanished into the darkness once his task was done. By the end of the week, every mailbox on the block had disappeared. That's when I realized—it wasn't the mailbox he feared... it was what was coming in the mail he wanted to hide...

My boyfriend begged me to watch the latest horror movie, fully aware that I scare way too easily. What I didn't know was that he and his best friend, Kyle, had cooked up a prank to frighten me during the scariest scene. The movie was called Live Fear, and its whole gimmick was that it felt so real, you'd forget you were watching fiction. But what none of us knew was that Live Fear wasn't just a movie—it was alive, and it fed off screams. Right on cue, Kyle banged on the window, and I let out a blood-curdling scream. That's when the screen glitched—and something stepped out of the static.

Mr. Dobbs' senior ethics class had been secretly planning a mission for weeks—to rescue the hamsters used in animal testing at Pharmcore Labs. They believed the treatment of the tiny creatures was inhumane, and their protest would come in the form of anonymous liberation and destruction. Under the cover of night, they snuck into the facility and made their way to the animal cages, quietly opening latches and setting the hamsters free. But just as they neared the final row, strange sounds echoed from the back corridor—soft, mechanical whirring mixed with muffled squeaks. Most of the students panicked and fled, but two stayed behind, drawn to the noise. When they opened the red door...

The plan was simple—get in, grab the valuables, get out. The house was massive, tucked behind iron gates and hedges, the kind of place rich people only live in on weekends. The burglar slipped through an unlocked window, silent and focused, until they started noticing strange details: portraits where the eyes seemed to follow, rooms kept ice-cold despite the summer heat, and a locked study with books too new for anyone to have read. Behind a bookcase, they discovered a secret room—and inside, a 24-karat gold coffin lay in the center, its value beyond comprehension. But what did it hold? As they moved the lid, the smell of sulfur filled the air...

Tully and Sully, a pair of grouper fish, lived peacefully in a vibrant mangrove reef—a harmonious underwater community where every species moved in perfect rhythm. Life was calm, colorful, and safe. But one morning, the water shifted. It turned red, thick with the scent of blood. Out of the murky distance, a school of hybrid piranha burst through the reef—razor-toothed, fast, and swarming the once tranquil cove. They weren't just looking for a new home... they were after a snack and Sully was first on the menu...

Two fairy godmothers, once cordial acquaintances, had found themselves locked in a silent feud—each determined that her goddaughter would win the heart of the kingdom's only prince. It started subtly: a shimmer in the hair, a sparkle in the eyes, a voice that sang like wind chimes. But soon, the spells escalated. One cast a charm for irresistible laughter, the other a glamour for flawless elegance. Back and forth they went, layering enchantments like armor, until their goddaughters no longer recognized themselves in the mirror. On the night of the royal ball, both young women stepped onto the palace steps glowing with unnatural perfection. As the Prince appeared he took one look and...

Erica loved playing in her mom's closet—shoes, clothes, and accessories piled up, everything a teenager could dream of. While digging through a stack of high heels in the corner, she stumbled upon something strange: a hidden lever built into the wall. Curiosity got the better of her, and when she pulled it, a trap door creaked open in the floor, revealing a narrow ladder leading into darkness. Without hesitation, she climbed down—and found herself in a hidden bunker lined with maps, weapons, and dossiers filled with photos and detailed notes on potential targets. Her heart pounded as the truth set in—her mom was either an agent or an assassin... but working for who? Before she could process it, she heard the front door open and her mom's voice calling her name—just as the trap door reset and sealed shut above her.

COSTUME
ROOM

Our school was set to put on the musical Cats, and I had the daunting task of creating most of the costumes. The irony? I'm allergic to cats—and honestly, I've never liked them. But our drama teacher, who was equal parts eccentric and dramatic, insisted the costumes look as realistic as possible. One late night, while finishing up in the costume room, I headed toward the door—only for it to slam shut and lock from the outside. I pounded on it, but no one answered. Then, from an upper window, I heard a creak... and saw someone begin pouring in live cats by the dozens. My allergies flared instantly—eyes burning, chest tightening, breath shortening. As I slumped to the floor, fading fast, I started to see images of...

It started as a soft tapping outside my bedroom window—barely noticeable at first. I figured it was just a woodpecker, harmless and routine. But night after night, the tapping returned, always in the same slow, steady rhythm, always just as I was about to fall asleep. Then I began hearing it during the day, even when no bird was in sight. Without realizing it, I started to lose time—hours slipping by as I stared at the window, listening, waiting. It wasn't just noise anymore; it was a pattern, pulling me in. One morning, I woke to find the woodpecker perched on my windowsill, its eyes locked with mine, tapping in that same exact rhythm. I fell this hypnotic trance fall over me then I realized...

The full moon hung high and bright as our hayride bumped along the edge of the cornfield, the wagon creaking beneath us and the tractor chugging steadily ahead. Everyone was laughing, bundled in blankets, sipping cider—until we reached the woods. That's when the bats appeared. At first just a few, darting through the trees. Then dozens, maybe hundreds, diving low over the wagon like something had disturbed them. The horses reared and the tractor stalled. In the sudden silence, one bat broke away from the swarm and hovered inches from my face—its eyes glowing faintly red. Then...

Working at the local candy store after school was usually quiet—until the evening a herd of tiny goats wandered in from the alley behind the shop. I had no idea where they came from, and neither did anyone else. They were oddly silent, their little hooves clicking on the tile as they moved in perfect unison. As I tried to herd them out, one reared up and knocked over the giant gumball display, sending thousands of gumballs scattering across the floor. That's when I noticed it—carved into the bottom of each gumball was a strange symbol, like a tiny rune. The goats froze, turned toward me, and all at once...

Piccadilly®